The AI Ascension

*Harnessing the Power of
Artificial Intelligence for
Universal Empowerment*

Theodore Bristol

CONTENTS

Title Page
I. Introduction	1
II. Understanding AI	5
III. AI in Daily Life	13
IV. AI in Business and Industry	22
V. AI for Creativity and Innovation	33
VI. AI and the Future of Work	45
VII. Ethical Considerations and Challenges	53
VIII. Preparing for an AI-Driven World	63
IX. Case Studies and Success Stories	73
X. Conclusion	82

I. INTRODUCTION

A. The advent of AI and its growing importance

In the tapestry of human history, few innovations have captivated our collective imagination and held the potential to reshape our world as profoundly as Artificial Intelligence (AI). From ancient philosophers' earliest musings to modern-day technologists' bold visions, the quest to create intelligent machines has been an enduring fascination. Today, we stand at the precipice of an AI revolution, witnessing the rapid proliferation of intelligent systems transforming industries, reshaping societies, and redefining what it means to be human.

The advent of AI marks a pivotal moment in our journey as a species. It is a testament to our unrelenting curiosity, boundless creativity, and unwavering determination to push the boundaries of what is possible. AI is not merely a technological advancement; it manifests our deepest aspirations and reflects our most cherished values. It embodies our desire to create, explore, and understand the world around us in ever-greater depth and detail.

As we embark on this exhilarating journey into the era of AI, we are confronted with many possibilities and challenges. The rise of intelligent machines raises fundamental questions about the nature of intelligence, the future of work, and what it means to be human. It demands that we grapple with complex ethical dilemmas, navigate uncharted territories, and forge new paths in a world where the lines between human and machine are increasingly blurred.

Yet, amidst the uncertainty and the upheaval, there lies an unparalleled opportunity. AI has the power to unleash human potential in ways we have never before imagined. It can catalyze innovation, a tool for empowerment, and a force for positive change. By harnessing the power of AI, we can tackle the most pressing challenges of our time, from climate change and disease eradication to poverty alleviation and educational access. We can create a world where every individual, regardless of their background or circumstances, has the opportunity to thrive and reach their full potential.

B. The purpose of this book: to explore AI's potential for empowering individuals

This book is an invitation to embark on a journey of discovery and empowerment. It is a call to action for everyone, regardless of their technical expertise or professional background, to explore AI's transformative potential and harness its power for personal and collective growth. Through the pages of this book, we will demystify the complex world of AI, breaking down its concepts, applications, and implications in a way that is accessible, engaging, and empowering.

Our aim is not merely to provide a technical overview of AI but to paint a vivid picture of how this technology can be leveraged to enhance every aspect of our lives. We will explore how to transform industries, from healthcare and education to finance and entertainment, and envision the countless possibilities. We will delve into AI's ethical considerations and challenges and provide a framework for navigating this uncharted territory with wisdom, compassion, and foresight.

Most importantly, this book celebrates human potential. It is a testament to our resilience, adaptability, and boundless capacity for growth and transformation. By harnessing the power of AI, we can amplify our abilities, expand our horizons, and create a world where every individual has the opportunity to thrive and make a meaningful impact.

So, dear reader, I invite you to embark on this journey with an open mind, a curious heart, and a steadfast commitment to personal and collective empowerment. Together, let us explore the frontiers of AI and discover how this transformative technology can help us build a brighter, more equitable, and more abundant future for all.

II. UNDERSTANDING AI

A. What is Artificial Intelligence?

Artificial Intelligence, or AI, is a term that has captured the imagination of people worldwide. But what exactly is AI? At its core, AI refers to developing computer systems that can perform tasks that typically require human intelligence, such as visual perception, speech recognition, decision-making, and language translation. It is the creation of machines that can think, learn, and adapt, mimicking the cognitive functions of the human mind.

AI is not a monolithic entity but rather a constellation of technologies and approaches that work together to create intelligent systems. These include machine learning, deep learning, natural language processing, computer vision, and robotics. Each subfield contributes to the overarching goal of creating machines that can perceive, reason, and act in ways that are similar to, or even surpass, human capabilities.

One of AI's key characteristics is its ability to learn from data. Unlike traditional computer programs that rely on explicit instructions and predetermined rules, AI systems can learn from experience, adapting and improving their performance over time. This learning can be supervised, where the system is trained on labeled data, or unsupervised, where it discovers patterns and relationships independently.

Another defining feature of AI is its ability to handle complexity and uncertainty. In an increasingly interconnected and data-driven world, AI systems can process vast amounts of information, identify patterns and insights, and make decisions in real-time. This enables them to tackle problems too complex or dynamic for traditional computational approaches.

B. The history and evolution of AI

The quest to create intelligent machines is not a new one. The idea of AI can be traced back to ancient myths and legends, from the talking statues of ancient Greece to the golems of Jewish folklore. However, in the mid-20th century, AI emerged as a formal field of study.

"Artificial Intelligence" was first coined in 1956 by computer scientist John McCarthy, who defined it as "the science and engineering of making intelligent machines." In the following decades, AI research progressed in fits and starts, with periods of great optimism followed by periods of disillusionment and reduced funding, known as "AI winters."

One of the earliest milestones in AI was Warren McCulloch and Walter Pitts's development of the first neural network in 1943. This laid the foundation for machine learning, which would become one of the most important subfields of AI. In the 1950s and 1960s, AI researchers developed the first AI programs, including the Logic Theorist and the General Problem Solver, which could solve mathematical problems and play chess.

The 1970s and 1980s saw the emergence of expert systems, which used rule-based reasoning to mimic the decision-making of human experts in specific domains, such as medicine and engineering. However, these early AI systems were limited by their reliance on hand-crafted rules and the inability to learn from data.

The 1990s and 2000s saw a resurgence of interest in AI, driven by machine learning advances and large dataset availability. The development of deep understanding, a subfield of machine learning that uses neural networks with many layers, led to breakthroughs in computer vision, speech recognition, and natural language processing.

Today, AI is a rapidly evolving field, transforming industries and reshaping societies. From self-driving cars and personalized medicine to intelligent assistants and autonomous robots, AI is becoming increasingly integrated into our daily lives, with the potential to revolutionize how we live, work, and interact with the world around us.

C. Types of AI: Narrow, General, and Super AI

AI is not a monolithic entity but a spectrum of capabilities ranging from narrow, task-specific systems to hypothetical superintelligent machines that can outperform humans in any cognitive task. Understanding the different types of AI is crucial for navigating the complex landscape of this rapidly evolving field.

The most common type of AI today is narrow or weak AI. These systems are designed to perform a specific task, such as image recognition, speech transcription, or language translation. Narrow AI systems are trained on large datasets and use machine learning algorithms to learn patterns and make predictions within their specific domain. While these systems can outperform humans in their particular tasks, they are limited in their scope and cannot generalize their knowledge to other domains.

General AI, strong AI, or human-level AI refers to hypothetical machines that can perform any intellectual task that a human can. These systems could reason, plan, learn, and adapt to new situations like a human mind. While significant advances in AI have been made in recent years, we still need to achieve general AI. Creating machines that match the human mind's flexibility, creativity, and common-sense reasoning remains a grand challenge for AI researchers.

Beyond general AI lies the concept of superintelligence or super AI. This refers to hypothetical machines that surpass human intelligence in every cognitive domain, from scientific discovery and artistic creation to strategic planning and social skills. The development of superintelligent AI is a topic of much speculation and debate, with some experts warning of the potential risks and challenges of creating machines that are vastly more intelligent than humans.

It is important to note that the boundaries between these different types of AI are not always clear-cut, and there is ongoing debate and research on how to define and measure intelligence in machines. Moreover, as AI systems become more sophisticated and integrated into our daily lives, the distinctions between narrow, general, and super AI may blur, raising new ethical, social, and philosophical questions about the nature of intelligence and the relationship between humans and machines.

D. Current state of AI technology

AI is a rapidly evolving field, with breakthroughs and applications emerging unprecedentedly. In recent years, AI has made significant strides in various domains, from healthcare and finance to transportation and entertainment. Here are some of the most notable developments in AI technology today:

* Machine Learning: Machine learning is the backbone of modern AI, enabling systems to learn from data and improve their performance over time. Recent advances in deep learning, a subfield of machine learning that uses neural networks with many layers, have led to breakthroughs in computer vision, speech recognition, and natural language processing.

* Computer Vision: AI systems can now perform tasks such as object recognition, facial recognition, and scene understanding with remarkable accuracy. This has led to applications in autonomous vehicles, security and surveillance, and medical imaging.

* Natural Language Processing: AI systems can now understand, generate, and translate human language increasingly sophisticatedly. This has led to the development of intelligent assistants, chatbots, and automated writing tools that can engage in natural conversations and perform complex language tasks.

* Robotics: AI enables the development of intelligent robots that can perceive, plan, and act in complex environments. From industrial robots in manufacturing to autonomous drones and self-

driving cars, AI is transforming the field of robotics and creating new opportunities for automation and efficiency.

* Generative Models: AI can now generate realistic images, videos, and music, blurring the lines between human and machine creativity. Generative models such as GANs (Generative Adversarial Networks) and transformers have opened up new content creation and personalization possibilities.

Despite these impressive advances, AI technology still faces significant challenges and limitations. One of the biggest challenges is more transparency and interpretability in many AI systems' intense learning models. This has led to concerns about bias, fairness, and accountability in AI decision-making.

Another challenge is the need for high-quality data to train AI systems. This can be particularly difficult in domains such as healthcare, where data privacy and security are paramount. Moreover, the current state of AI is still predominantly narrow and task-specific, and we are still far from achieving general AI that can match the flexibility and adaptability of the human mind.

As AI evolves and becomes more integrated into our daily lives, we must develop a deeper understanding of its capabilities, limitations, and implications. This requires ongoing research, collaboration, and dialogue between AI researchers, policymakers, and the broader public. By working together, we can harness the power of AI to create a more intelligent, efficient, and equitable world while ensuring that it is developed and used responsibly and ethically.

III. AI IN DAILY LIFE

A. AI-powered personal assistants

Imagine having a tireless, ever-present companion ready to assist you with any task, answer any question, and cater to your every need. This is the promise of AI-powered personal assistants, rapidly becoming ubiquitous daily. From smartphones and smart speakers to wearables and automobiles, these intelligent agents transform how we interact with technology and the world around us.

At the heart of every AI-powered personal assistant lies a sophisticated natural language processing system that can understand and respond to human speech and text. These systems use machine learning algorithms to continuously improve their language understanding and generation capabilities, allowing them to engage in increasingly natural and contextual conversations.

One of the most familiar examples of an AI-powered personal assistant is Apple's Siri, which first appeared on the iPhone in 2011. Since then, other major tech companies have followed suit, introducing intelligent assistants, such as Google

Assistant, Amazon's Alexa, and Microsoft's Cortana. These assistants can perform various tasks, from setting reminders and alarms to playing music, providing weather and traffic updates, and even controlling smart home devices.

However, the capabilities of AI-powered personal assistants extend far beyond simple voice commands and queries. With the integration of machine learning and natural language processing, these systems can now engage in more complex and open-ended conversations, providing personalized recommendations, offering emotional support, and even cracking jokes.

Moreover, as these assistants integrate into our daily routines, they learn to anticipate our needs and preferences, proactively offering suggestions and insights to help us navigate our busy lives. For example, an AI-powered assistant might remind you to leave early for a meeting due to heavy traffic or suggest a nearby restaurant based on your previous dining preferences.

As AI-powered personal assistants continue to evolve and become more sophisticated, they have the potential to revolutionize the way we live and work. By offloading routine tasks and decision-making to intelligent machines, we can free up our time and cognitive resources to focus on more meaningful and creative pursuits. At the same time, the increasing reliance on AI assistants raises important questions about privacy, security, and the long-term effects of outsourcing our cognitive functions to machines.

B. AI in smartphones and smart homes

AI is not just confined to personal assistants; it is becoming increasingly integrated into the devices and environments that surround us. Smartphones and smart homes are two of the most prominent examples of this trend.

Smartphones have become the primary interface through which we interact with AI daily. From facial recognition and voice assistants to predictive text and app recommendations, AI is woven into the very fabric of the modern smartphone experience. Machine learning algorithms optimize battery life, improve camera performance, and personalize content and notifications based on our usage patterns.

However, the impact of AI on smartphones extends beyond individual devices. With the rise of edge computing and 5G networks, smartphones can perform complex AI tasks locally without needing cloud processing. This enables new applications in augmented reality, real-time language translation, and on-device machine learning.

Smart homes are another domain where AI is rapidly transforming our lives. With the proliferation of internet-connected devices and sensors, our homes are becoming increasingly intelligent and autonomous. AI-powered systems can now automate temperature control, lighting, and security tasks, learning our preferences and adapting to our routines over time.

One of the most promising applications of AI in smart homes is energy management. By analyzing data from smart meters, weather forecasts, and occupancy sensors, AI algorithms can optimize energy consumption and reduce waste, leading to significant cost savings and environmental benefits.

AI is also enabling new forms of home entertainment and interaction. Smart speakers and displays with built-in AI assistants can be hubs for controlling other devices, playing media, and providing information and entertainment. Meanwhile, AI-powered robots and appliances are beginning to enter the home, offering new levels of convenience and automation.

As AI becomes more integrated into our smartphones and smart homes, it is vital to consider privacy, security, and user control implications. While these technologies offer tremendous benefits in terms of convenience and efficiency, they also raise concerns about data collection, surveillance, and the erosion of personal autonomy. As we move forward, it will be crucial to develop standards and regulations that balance the benefits of AI with the need to protect individual rights and freedoms.

C. AI in education and learning

Education is one of the most promising and consequential domains for the application of AI. With the ability to personalize learning, automate assessment, and provide intelligent tutoring, AI can transform how we teach and learn, making education more effective, efficient, and accessible.

One of AI's key benefits in education is its ability to personalize learning experiences based on individual needs and preferences. AI algorithms can dynamically adapt instructional content and pacing to optimize learning outcomes by analyzing student performance, engagement, and learning styles. This helps address the limitations of traditional one-size-fits-all approaches to education, ensuring that each student receives the support and challenge they need to succeed.

AI is also being used to automate the process of assessment and feedback. With the help of natural language processing and machine learning, AI systems can now grade essays, provide feedback on writing style and grammar, and even detect plagiarism. This not only saves time and reduces the burden on teachers but also enables more frequent and consistent feedback, helping students to identify areas for improvement and track their progress over time.

Another promising application of AI in education is intelligent tutoring systems. These systems use natural language processing and machine learning to provide personalized, one-on-one instruction and support, mimicking the role of a human tutor. By analyzing student responses and adapting to individual learning needs, intelligent tutoring systems can provide targeted feedback, hints, and explanations, helping students to master complex concepts and skills.

Beyond the classroom, AI also transforms how we learn and acquire knowledge in informal settings. With the rise of online learning platforms and MOOCs (massive open online courses), AI is used to recommend courses, track progress, and provide personalized feedback and support. Meanwhile, AI-powered chatbots and virtual assistants provide on-demand educational content and answer questions, making learning more accessible and convenient.

As AI continues to advance, it has the potential to democratize education and make high-quality learning experiences available to everyone, regardless of their background or location. At the same time, the increasing use of AI in education raises important questions about privacy, bias, and the role of human teachers and mentors. As we progress, it will be essential to develop ethical and responsible approaches to using AI in education, ensuring that it enhances and supports human learning rather than replaces it.

D. AI in healthcare and wellness

Healthcare is one of the most critical and challenging domains for AI applications. With the ability to analyze vast amounts of medical data, assist with diagnosis and treatment planning, and even perform surgical procedures, AI has the potential to revolutionize the way we prevent, detect, and treat disease.

One of the most promising applications of AI in healthcare is medical imaging. With the help of deep learning algorithms, AI systems can now analyze medical images such as X-rays, CT scans, and MRIs with remarkable accuracy, detecting subtle abnormalities and patterns that the human eye might miss. This improves the speed and accuracy of diagnosis and frees radiologists to focus on more complex and nuanced cases.

AI is also being used to assist with drug discovery and development. AI algorithms can identify promising drug targets and predict potential side effects and interactions by analyzing vast amounts of biomedical data, including genetic information and clinical trial results. This can accelerate the drug development process, reduce costs, and bring new treatments to market faster.

Another important application of AI in healthcare is personalized medicine. By analyzing individual patient data, including genetic information, medical history, and lifestyle factors, AI algorithms can help predict disease risk, optimize treatment plans, and even design customized therapies based on a patient's unique genetic profile. This can transform how we approach disease prevention and treatment, moving from a one-size-fits-all approach to a more targeted and effective model.

Beyond the clinical setting, AI is also being used to promote health and wellness in everyday life. Wearable devices and smartphone apps powered by AI can track our physical activity, sleep patterns, and vital signs, providing personalized recommendations and feedback to help us maintain optimal health. Meanwhile, AI-powered chatbots and virtual assistants offer mental health support and counseling, making these services more accessible and affordable.

As AI becomes more integrated into healthcare and wellness, it raises important ethical and societal questions. While the potential benefits are enormous, there are also concerns about privacy, security, and the potential for bias and discrimination in AI-powered healthcare systems. Moreover, the increasing reliance on AI in healthcare raises questions about the role of human healthcare providers and the importance of empathy, compassion, and human connection in the healing process.

As we progress, developing responsible and inclusive approaches to using AI in healthcare will be crucial. We must ensure that it enhances and supports human expertise rather than replaces it. This will require ongoing collaboration and dialogue between healthcare providers, researchers, policymakers, and the public as we work together to harness the power of AI to improve health outcomes and quality of life for all.

IV. AI IN BUSINESS AND INDUSTRY

A. AI-driven automation and efficiency

In the fast-paced world of business and industry, the ability to streamline processes, reduce costs, and maximize efficiency is critical to success. AI-driven automation is revolutionizing how companies operate and compete in the global marketplace.

One of the most significant advantages of AI-driven automation is its ability to handle repetitive, time-consuming tasks with unparalleled speed and accuracy. By leveraging machine learning algorithms and robotic process automation (RPA), businesses can automate various processes, from data entry and document processing to supply chain management and quality control. This saves time, reduces human error risk, and frees employees to focus on more strategic and creative tasks.

Moreover, AI-driven automation enables businesses to operate 24/7 without needing breaks, vacations, or sick leave. This can lead to significant improvements in productivity and output, allowing companies to meet the ever-increasing demands of customers and stakeholders.

However, the benefits of AI-driven automation extend far beyond simple cost savings and efficiency gains. By analyzing vast amounts of data in real time, AI algorithms can help businesses identify patterns, predict trends, and make data-driven decisions quickly and accurately. This can lead to better resource allocation, improved forecasting, and more agile decision-making, giving companies a competitive edge in an increasingly dynamic and unpredictable business landscape.

As AI-driven automation becomes more sophisticated and ubiquitous, it transforms industries from manufacturing and logistics to healthcare and finance. In the manufacturing sector, for example, AI-powered robots assemble products, inspect quality, and optimize production lines, leading to faster, more efficient, and more consistent output. Meanwhile, AI algorithms are used in the logistics industry to optimize routes, predict demand, and streamline supply chain operations, reducing costs and improving delivery times.

However, the rise of AI-driven automation also raises important questions about the future of work and the role of human employees. As machines become increasingly capable of performing tasks that were once the exclusive domain of humans, there are concerns about job displacement and the need for worker retraining and upskilling. At the same time, the increasing reliance on AI systems raises questions about transparency, accountability, and the potential for bias and discrimination in automated decision-making.

As we move forward, it will be crucial for businesses to develop responsible and inclusive approaches to using AI-driven automation, ensuring that it augments and supports human capabilities rather than entirely replacing them. This will require ongoing dialogue and collaboration between business leaders, policymakers, and the broader public as we work to harness the power of AI to drive innovation, growth, and shared prosperity.

B. AI in customer service and support

In today's hyper-competitive business landscape, exceptional customer service and support are no longer excellent; they are a fundamental requirement for success. AI is significantly impacting this area, transforming how companies interact with their customers and delivering value at every touchpoint.

One of the most visible applications of AI in customer service is chatbots and virtual assistants. Powered by natural language processing and machine learning, these AI-driven tools can handle various customer inquiries and support requests, from answering basic questions and providing product information to troubleshooting technical issues and processing orders. This improves the speed and efficiency of customer service and enables companies to offer 24/7 support, meeting customers' needs across different time zones and geographies.

However, the benefits of AI in customer service extend far beyond simple automation and cost savings. By analyzing vast amounts of customer data, including purchase history, browsing behavior, and social media activity, AI algorithms can help companies better understand customers' needs, preferences, and pain points. This can lead to more personalized and proactive support and targeted marketing and product recommendations that drive customer loyalty and retention.

Moreover, AI-powered sentiment analysis and emotion recognition can help companies quickly detect and respond to customer frustration and dissatisfaction, preventing minor issues from escalating into major problems. By analyzing the tone and content of customer interactions across multiple channels, including phone, email, and social media, AI algorithms can identify patterns and trends in customer sentiment, enabling companies to address concerns and improve the overall customer experience proactively.

As AI advances, it opens up new customer service and support possibilities. For example, AI-powered visual search and image recognition can help customers find products more efficiently. At the same time, virtual try-on and augmented reality experiences can provide more immersive and engaging ways to explore and purchase products. Meanwhile, AI-driven predictive maintenance and remote monitoring can help companies identify and resolve issues before they impact customers, reducing downtime and improving overall reliability and performance.

However, the increasing use of AI in customer service also raises important questions about privacy, security, and the role of human employees. As companies collect and analyze more customer data, there are concerns about how that data is being used and protected, as well as the potential for bias and discrimination in AI-powered decision-making. Moreover, as AI systems become more sophisticated and autonomous, there are questions about human oversight and intervention and the importance of empathy, creativity, and personal connection in delivering exceptional customer experiences.

As we progress, companies must develop responsible and customer-centric approaches to using AI in customer service and support. This will require ongoing investment in AI technologies and talent and a commitment to transparency, accountability, and continuous improvement in delivering customer value.

C. AI in marketing and advertising

In the fast-paced, data-driven marketing and advertising world, AI is quickly becoming indispensable for reaching and engaging customers at scale. By leveraging machine learning algorithms and predictive analytics, companies can gain deeper insights into customer behavior, preferences, and intent, enabling more targeted and effective marketing campaigns that drive business growth and profitability.

One of the most significant applications of AI in marketing is programmatic advertising. This involves using AI algorithms to automate the buying and placement of digital ads in real-time based on a wide range of data points, including demographics, interests, and past browsing behavior. Programmatic advertising can help companies reach the right customers with the right message at the right time, reducing ad spend and improving overall return on investment (ROI) by optimizing ad targeting and bidding strategies in real-time.

AI is also transforming the way companies approach content creation and personalization. AI algorithms can help marketers identify the most effective content formats, themes, and messaging for different audience segments by analyzing vast customer data, including social media activity, purchase history, and website interactions. This can lead to more relevant and engaging content experiences that drive higher customer engagement, conversion, and loyalty.

Moreover, AI-powered chatbots and virtual assistants are becoming increasingly popular tools for customer engagement and lead generation. By providing instant, personalized responses to customer inquiries and support requests, these AI-driven tools can help companies build stronger customer relationships while freeing up human employees to focus on more complex and strategic tasks.

Another important application of AI in marketing is predictive analytics. By analyzing historical data and identifying patterns and trends, AI algorithms can help companies predict future customer behavior and market trends with unprecedented accuracy. This can lead to more proactive and data-driven decision-making and more effective demand forecasting, inventory management, and resource allocation.

As AI advances, it opens up new possibilities for marketing and advertising innovation. For example, AI-powered image and video recognition can help companies analyze and optimize visual content for maximum impact. In contrast, natural language processing and sentiment analysis can help marketers better understand and respond to real-time customer feedback and opinions.

However, the increasing use of AI in marketing and advertising also raises important ethical and societal questions. There are concerns about privacy and data security, as well as the potential for bias and discrimination in AI-powered marketing decisions. Moreover, the increasing sophistication and pervasiveness of AI-driven marketing techniques raise questions about the impact on consumer choice and autonomy and the need for greater transparency and accountability in using these powerful technologies.

As we progress, companies must develop responsible and customer-centric approaches to using AI in marketing and advertising. This will require ongoing investment in AI technologies and talent, as well as a commitment to transparency, fairness, and continuous improvement in the delivery of marketing value.

D. AI in finance and investment

The world of finance and investment is no stranger to the transformative power of technology. From the rise of electronic trading and algorithmic investing to the emergence of digital currencies and blockchain, the financial industry has always been at the forefront of technological innovation.

Today, AI is taking this innovation to new heights, revolutionizing how financial institutions operate, invest, and serve their customers.

Risk management and fraud detection are two of the most significant applications of AI in finance. By analyzing vast amounts of financial data, including transaction histories, market trends, and customer behavior, AI algorithms can help financial institutions identify potential risks and anomalies in real time. This can lead to more proactive and effective risk management strategies and reduce fraud and economic crime losses.

AI is also transforming the way financial institutions approach investment and portfolio management. By leveraging machine learning algorithms and predictive analytics, AI-powered investment platforms can help investors identify promising investment opportunities, optimize portfolio allocations, and manage risk more effectively. This can lead to higher returns, lower investor costs, and more data-driven and objective investment decision-making.

Another important application of AI in finance is customer service and support. By leveraging natural language processing and machine learning, financial institutions can develop AI-powered chatbots and virtual assistants to provide instant, personalized customer support across various financial products and services. This can improve the speed and efficiency of customer service, freeing human employees to focus on more complex and high-value tasks.

AI is also enabling new forms of financial innovation and inclusion. For example, AI-powered credit scoring and underwriting algorithms can help financial institutions assess the creditworthiness of previously underserved or unbanked populations, opening up new economic access and empowerment opportunities. Meanwhile, AI-driven robo-advisors and automated investment platforms are making it easier and more affordable for individuals to access professional investment advice and services, regardless of their wealth or financial sophistication.

As AI continues to evolve, it will likely have an even more significant impact on the financial industry in the coming years. For example, AI-powered algorithms could help optimize capital allocation and risk management across entire economies while enabling new financial modeling and simulation forms. Meanwhile, the increasing integration of AI with other emerging technologies, such as blockchain and the Internet of Things, could lead to entirely new financial products, services, and business models.

However, the increasing use of AI in finance also raises important ethical and regulatory questions. There are concerns about the potential for bias and discrimination in AI-powered financial decision-making and the need for greater transparency and accountability in using these powerful technologies. Moreover, the increasing reliance on AI in the financial industry could have significant implications for job displacement and the need for worker retraining and upskilling.

As we move forward, it will be crucial for financial institutions and regulators to work together to develop responsible and inclusive approaches to using AI in finance. This will require ongoing investment in AI technologies and talent and a commitment to transparency, fairness, and continuous improvement in delivering financial value. By harnessing the power of AI responsibly and ethically, the financial industry can drive innovation and growth and promote greater financial inclusion and empowerment for all.

V. AI FOR CREATIVITY AND INNOVATION

A. AI-assisted art and design

In the realm of creativity and innovation, AI is opening up new frontiers and possibilities, challenging our assumptions about the nature of artistic expression and the role of technology in the creative process. One of the most exciting applications of AI in this domain is in the field of art and design, where AI algorithms are being used to generate, manipulate, and enhance visual content in once unimaginable ways.

Tools like generative adversarial networks (GANs) and style transfer algorithms are at the forefront of this AI-assisted art revolution. GANs are machine learning algorithms that can generate new images and designs based on patterns and features learned from existing data sets. By training in vast collections of artwork, photographs, and other visual media, GANs can create entirely new and original works of art that mimic the style and aesthetics of human artists.

On the other hand, style transfer algorithms allow users to apply one image or artwork's style and visual characteristics to another. This means that a photograph or video can be transformed to look like a painting by Van Gogh or Monet, or a 3D model can be stylized to resemble a sculpture by Rodin or Michelangelo. These tools enable new forms of artistic expression and experimentation, making it easier for designers and content creators to quickly and efficiently generate high-quality visual assets.

But AI's impact on art and design goes beyond generating new content. AI algorithms also analyze and understand visual aesthetics' underlying principles and patterns, allowing designers to make more informed and data-driven decisions about color, composition, and other design elements. This can lead to more effective and engaging visual communication and more personalized and targeted design experiences for different audiences and contexts.

Moreover, AI enables new collaboration and co-creation between humans and machines. For example, AI-powered design tools can suggest layout and color schemes based on user preferences and brand guidelines. At the same time, generative algorithms can create real-time variations and iterations of designs, allowing designers to explore and refine their ideas more quickly and effectively.

AI will likely have an even more significant impact on art and design as it advances. For example, AI-generated art and design could become more indistinguishable from human-created works, raising questions about authorship, originality, and the value of creativity in an age of artificial intelligence. Meanwhile, democratizing AI-assisted design tools could lead to new creative expression and innovation forms, empowering individuals and communities to tell their stories and shape their visual identities.

However, the increasing use of AI in art and design also raises important ethical and societal questions. There are concerns about the potential for bias and homogenization in AI-generated art and design and the need for greater transparency and accountability in using these powerful technologies. Moreover, the increasing automation of creative tasks could have significant implications for job displacement and the need for worker retraining and upskilling in the creative industries.

As we progress, it will be crucial for artists, designers, and technologists to work together to develop responsible and inclusive approaches to using AI in art and design. This will require ongoing investment in AI technologies and talent and a commitment to diversity, experimentation, continuous learning, and adaptation. By embracing AI's potential while recognizing its limitations and challenges, we can harness the power of this transformative technology to create new forms of beauty, meaning, and innovation in the world of art and design.

B. AI in music composition and generation

From the earliest days of computer-generated music in the 1950s to the latest advances in deep learning and neural networks, AI has been at the forefront of music composition and generation innovation. Today, AI algorithms are being used to create new musical styles, generate personalized playlists, and even compose entire songs and albums from scratch, opening up new possibilities for creativity, expression, and collaboration in the music industry.

One of the most exciting applications of AI in music is generative music, where algorithms create new musical compositions based on patterns and features learned from existing music data sets. By training in vast libraries of songs, genres, and musical styles, AI algorithms can generate entirely new and original pieces of music that mimic the characteristics and aesthetics of human composers and performers.

For example, AI-powered tools like Google's Magenta and IBM's Watson Beat can analyze a musical style or genre's structure, melody, and harmony and generate new compositions that adhere to those same patterns and rules. This means that an AI algorithm could create a new jazz standard, a classical symphony, or a pop song that sounds similar to the works of famous artists and composers but with unique variations and improvisations.

But AI is more than just being used to generate new music from scratch. It is also being used to enhance and manipulate existing music in new and creative ways. For example, AI-powered audio processing tools can automatically separate the different instruments and vocals in a song, allowing producers and remixers to isolate and manipulate specific elements of the music. Meanwhile, AI algorithms can analyze musical features' emotional and psychological impact, such as tempo, key, and timbre, allowing composers to create more targeted and effective musical experiences for various audiences and contexts.

Moreover, AI enables new forms of personalization and recommendation in the music industry. By analyzing user data and preferences, AI algorithms can generate personalized playlists and music recommendations tailored to individual tastes and moods. This helps users discover new music and artists they might like and allows music streaming services to provide more engaging and satisfying user experiences.

As AI continues to evolve, it will likely have an even more significant impact on music composition and generation. For example, AI-generated music could become more sophisticated and expressive, with the ability to convey complex emotions and narratives through sound. Meanwhile, integrating AI with other emerging technologies, such as virtual and augmented reality, could lead to entirely new musical experiences and interaction forms.

However, the increasing use of AI in music also raises important questions about creativity, authorship, and the role of human artists in an age of artificial intelligence. There are concerns about the potential for AI-generated music to replace or devalue the work of human composers and performers and the need for greater transparency and accountability in using these powerful technologies.

As we progress, it will be crucial for musicians, technologists, and policymakers to collaborate to develop responsible and inclusive approaches to using AI in music. This will require ongoing investment in AI technologies and talent and a commitment to experimentation, collaboration, continuous learning, and adaptation. By embracing the potential of AI while also recognizing its limitations and challenges, we can harness the power of this transformative technology to create new forms of musical expression, innovation, and cultural value.

C. AI in writing and storytelling

From the earliest days of computer-generated poetry in the 1960s to the latest advances in natural language processing and machine learning, AI has been at the forefront of innovation in writing and storytelling. Today, AI algorithms are being used to generate news articles, write creative fiction, and even develop entire storylines and characters for movies and TV shows, opening up new possibilities for creativity, expression, and collaboration in the literary and entertainment industries.

One of the most exciting applications of AI in writing is natural language generation, where algorithms create written content that is almost indistinguishable from human-written text. By training on vast data sets of books, articles, and other written works, AI algorithms can learn the patterns, structures, and styles of different forms of writing and then generate new text that mimics those same characteristics.

For example, AI-powered tools like GPT-3 and Grover can generate coherent and fluent text passages on almost any topic, from news articles and product descriptions to creative fiction and poetry. These tools can even be fine-tuned to mimic the writing style of specific authors or genres, allowing users to generate content that sounds like Shakespeare, Hemingway, or any other famous writer who wrote it.

But AI is more than just being used to generate text from scratch. It also assists and enhances human writing in new and creative ways. For example, AI-powered writing tools can suggest alternative word choices, correct grammar and spelling errors, and even provide feedback on a piece's clarity, coherence, and emotional impact. Meanwhile, AI algorithms can analyze the structure and pacing of a story or script, providing insights and suggestions for improving the narrative flow and keeping readers or viewers engaged.

Moreover, AI is enabling new forms of personalization and interactivity in storytelling. By analyzing user data and preferences, AI algorithms can generate customized stories and characters tailored to individual tastes and interests. This helps users discover new stories and worlds they might enjoy and allows writers and content creators to provide more engaging and satisfying user experiences.

As AI continues to evolve, it will likely have an even more significant impact on the world of writing and storytelling. For example, AI-generated stories could become more complex and nuanced, with the ability to incorporate multiple plotlines, characters, and themes. Meanwhile, integrating AI with other emerging technologies, such as virtual and augmented reality, could lead to entirely new immersive and interactive storytelling forms.

However, the increasing use of AI in writing also raises important questions about creativity, authorship, and the role of human writers in an age of artificial intelligence. There are concerns about the potential for AI-generated content to replace or devalue the work of human writers and journalists and the need for greater transparency and accountability in using these powerful technologies.

As we progress, it will be crucial for writers, technologists, and policymakers to work together to develop responsible and inclusive approaches to using AI in writing and storytelling. This will require ongoing investment in AI technologies and talent and a commitment to experimentation, collaboration, continuous learning, and adaptation. By embracing AI's potential while recognizing its limitations and challenges, we can harness the power of this transformative technology to create new forms of literary expression, innovation, and cultural value.

D. AI in problem-solving and ideation

Beyond artistic and creative expression, AI also transforms how we approach problem-solving and creativity in various domains, from business and engineering to science and social innovation. By leveraging the power of machine learning, data analysis, and computational creativity, AI algorithms are helping us to generate new ideas, identify hidden patterns and insights, and develop more effective and innovative solutions to complex challenges.

One of the most exciting applications of AI in problem-solving is in the field of generative design, where algorithms are used to explore vast design spaces and generate novel solutions that optimize for specific goals and constraints. By specifying the desired performance criteria and limitations of a design problem, such as weight, strength, cost, or aesthetics, AI algorithms can generate thousands or even millions of potential solutions that meet those criteria in unique and unexpected ways.

For example, AI-powered generative design tools like Autodesk's Dreamcatcher and Dassault Systèmes' 3DEXPERIENCE can help engineers and designers create new product designs that are lighter, stronger, and more efficient than traditional designs by exploring a much larger space of possibilities and configurations. Meanwhile, in fields like drug discovery and materials science, AI algorithms can help researchers identify new chemical compounds and molecular structures with specific desired properties, such as binding affinity, stability, or biocompatibility.

But AI is more than just being used to generate new solutions from scratch. It also enhances and augments human problem-solving and decision-making in new and powerful ways. For example,

AI-powered data analysis and visualization tools can help businesses and organizations identify patterns and trends in large and complex data sets, providing insights and recommendations for optimizing processes, reducing costs, or improving customer satisfaction. Meanwhile, AI algorithms can help individuals and teams break down complex problems into smaller, more manageable subproblems and identify the most promising solutions.

Moreover, AI enables new forms of collaborative and distributed problem-solving, where diverse groups of people and machines can work together to tackle shared challenges and generate collective intelligence. For example, AI-powered crowdsourcing platforms like Foldit and Eyewire can engage thousands of citizen scientists and gamers worldwide to solve complex scientific puzzles, such as protein folding and neuron mapping, by leveraging the power of human intuition and creativity alongside machine learning and data analysis.

As AI continues to evolve, it will likely have an even more significant impact on problem-solving and creativity. For example, AI algorithms could become more adept at understanding and modeling complex systems and phenomena, from climate change and economic markets to social networks and political dynamics. Meanwhile, integrating AI with other emerging technologies, such as blockchain and the Internet of Things, could enable new decentralized and self-organizing problem-solving networks that can adapt and evolve in response to changing conditions and needs.

However, the increasing use of AI in problem-solving also raises important questions about human agency, transparency, and accountability. There are concerns about the potential for AI-generated solutions to perpetuate or amplify existing biases and inequalities and the need for greater explainability and interpretability in AI decision-making processes. Moreover, the increasing automation of problem-solving tasks could significantly impact job displacement and the need for worker retraining and upskilling in many industries and professions.

As we move forward, it will be crucial for researchers, technologists, and policymakers to work together to develop responsible and inclusive approaches to using AI in problem-solving and creativity. This will require ongoing investment in AI technologies and talent and a commitment to interdisciplinary collaboration, ethical reflection, and continuous learning and adaptation. By embracing the potential of AI while also recognizing its limitations and challenges, we can harness the power of this transformative technology to create new forms of knowledge, innovation, and social impact that benefit all of humanity.

VI. AI AND THE FUTURE OF WORK

A. The impact of AI on job markets

As AI advances and permeates every aspect of our lives, one of the most pressing and controversial questions is how it will impact the future of work and employment. On one hand, AI has the potential to automate many routine and repetitive tasks, freeing up human workers to focus on more creative, strategic, and emotionally engaging work. On the other hand, there are growing concerns that AI could displace millions of workers across a wide range of industries, leading to widespread job losses, economic disruption, and social unrest.

To understand the impact of AI on job markets, it is essential to distinguish between different types of AI and their potential applications. Narrow or weak AI, designed to perform specific tasks within a limited domain, is already being used to automate many routine cognitive and manual tasks, from data entry and document processing to assembly line work and customer service.

While these applications of AI can undoubtedly improve efficiency and productivity, they also have the potential to displace many low-skilled and middle-skilled workers, particularly in sectors like manufacturing, retail, and transportation.

However, the impact of AI on job markets is about more than just automation and displacement. As AI becomes more sophisticated and ubiquitous, it creates new jobs and opportunities in data science, machine learning, and AI ethics and governance. Moreover, AI enables new forms of human-machine collaboration and augmentation, where humans and AI systems work together to achieve shared goals and outcomes. For example, AI algorithms can help doctors and teachers make more accurate diagnoses and personalized learning plans in healthcare and education while relying on human expertise and empathy to deliver high-quality care and support.

At the same time, it is essential to recognize that the benefits and risks of AI are uneven across different demographic groups and regions. Studies have shown that AI automation is likely to have a disproportionate impact on low-wage, low-skilled, and historically disadvantaged workers, including women, people of color, and those in developing countries. Moreover, the rapid pace of AI development and deployment creates new challenges for education and workforce development systems, which must adapt quickly to changing skill demands and job requirements.

B. Reskilling and upskilling for the AI era

To navigate the challenges and opportunities of the AI era, individuals, organizations, and societies must prioritize reskilling and upskilling initiatives to help workers adapt to new technologies and job markets. This means investing in education and training programs focusing on technical skills, such as data analysis and programming, and social and emotional skills, such as creativity, critical thinking, and collaboration.

One promising approach to reskilling and upskilling is to leverage the power of AI to create personalized and adaptive learning experiences that can help workers acquire new skills and knowledge at their own pace and in their context. For example, AI-powered learning platforms can use data on individual learning styles, preferences, and performance to recommend targeted content and exercises to help workers master specific competencies and domains. Meanwhile, AI algorithms can also identify skill gaps and job opportunities in real-time, assisting workers in navigating dynamic and uncertain job markets.

Another critical strategy for reskilling and upskilling is to foster greater collaboration and knowledge-sharing between industry, academia, and government. This means creating new partnerships and initiatives that can bring together diverse stakeholders to co-create and co-deliver training and education programs that are relevant, responsive, and inclusive. For example, companies can work with universities and community colleges to develop apprenticeship and internship programs that provide hands-on experience and mentorship for students and workers. Meanwhile, governments can provide funding and incentives for reskilling and upskilling initiatives that target underserved and at-risk populations.

C. Collaboration between humans and AI

As AI becomes more sophisticated and ubiquitous, it creates new opportunities for collaboration and synergy between humans and machines. Rather than viewing AI as a threat or replacement for human workers, we can think of AI as a tool and partner that can augment and enhance human capabilities in new and powerful ways.

One key area of human-AI collaboration is in the field of decision-making and problem-solving. By leveraging the power of machine learning and data analytics, AI systems can help humans make more informed and objective decisions while relying on human judgment and values to navigate complex trade-offs and ethical dilemmas. For example, AI algorithms can analyze vast amounts of data in finance and healthcare to identify patterns and risks humans might miss. In contrast, human experts can use their domain knowledge and intuition to interpret and act on those insights in context-specific ways.

Another critical area of human-AI collaboration is in the field of creativity and innovation. While AI algorithms can generate novel ideas and solutions by exploring vast combinatorial spaces, humans still need to provide the imagination, curiosity, and emotional intelligence that can guide and inspire those explorations. For example, in fields like art and music, AI algorithms can help human creators discover new styles, genres, and forms. In contrast, human artists can use their unique perspectives and experiences to imbue those creations with meaning and resonance.

Moreover, human-AI collaboration can also help to mitigate some of the risks and challenges associated with AI development and deployment. By involving human stakeholders in the design, testing, and governance of AI systems, we can ensure those systems are transparent, accountable, and aligned with human values and goals. For example, human oversight and input in fields like healthcare and criminal justice can help prevent AI bias and discrimination while ensuring that AI decisions are explainable and contestable.

D. Entrepreneurship opportunities in the age of AI

Finally, the age of AI is also creating new

opportunities for entrepreneurship and innovation across a wide range of industries and domains. As AI technologies become more accessible and affordable, entrepreneurs and startups can leverage the power of machine learning and data analytics to create new products, services, and business models that can disrupt traditional markets and create value for customers and society.

One key area of AI entrepreneurship is in the field of healthcare and wellness. Using AI algorithms to analyze patient data and medical records, startups can develop personalized treatment plans and predictive models to improve patient outcomes and reduce healthcare costs. For example, companies like Babylon Health and Ada Health are using AI chatbots and symptom checkers to provide accessible and affordable primary care to millions of users worldwide. Meanwhile, startups like Recursion Pharmaceuticals and BenevolentAI use AI to accelerate drug discovery and development by identifying new therapeutic targets and molecules that can treat complex diseases.

Another important area of AI entrepreneurship is education and learning. Using AI algorithms to personalize and adapt learning experiences, startups can help students and workers acquire new skills and knowledge more efficiently and effectively. For example, companies like Duolingo and Coursera are using AI to create interactive and gamified language learning and online education platforms that can reach millions of learners worldwide. Meanwhile, startups like Knewton and Carnegie Learning use AI to develop adaptive learning systems that tailor content and feedback to individual student needs and preferences.

Moreover, AI entrepreneurship also creates new opportunities for social and environmental impact. By using AI algorithms to analyze social and ecological data, startups can develop new solutions and interventions that can address complex global challenges, from climate change and biodiversity loss to poverty and inequality. For example, companies like Orbital Insight and Descartes Labs use AI and satellite imagery to monitor deforestation and land use change. In contrast, startups like Aclima and ClimaCell use AI and sensor networks to map real-time air pollution and weather patterns.

Of course, AI entrepreneurship comes with risks and challenges, from data privacy and security concerns to algorithmic bias and accountability issues. To navigate these challenges, entrepreneurs and startups must prioritize responsible and ethical AI development and deployment by engaging with diverse stakeholders, following best practices and standards, and being transparent and responsive to public concerns and feedback.

As we move into the age of AI, it is clear that the complex interplay of technological, economic, and social forces will shape the future of work and entrepreneurship. By embracing the opportunities and challenges of AI and by prioritizing reskilling, collaboration, and innovation, we can create a future of work that is more inclusive, empowering, and fulfilling for all. Whether as workers, entrepreneurs, or citizens, we all have a role in shaping the future of AI and its impact on our lives and societies.

VII. ETHICAL CONSIDERATIONS AND CHALLENGES

A. Bias and fairness in AI systems

As AI systems become increasingly integrated into our daily lives, making decisions that impact everything from hiring and lending to criminal justice and healthcare, ensuring fairness and mitigating bias is paramount. AI algorithms are only as unbiased as the data they are trained on and the humans who design them. AI systems can perpetuate and even amplify discrimination if the training data reflects historical biases or the algorithms are designed with inherent prejudices.

One prominent example of AI bias is in facial recognition technology. Studies have shown that some facial recognition algorithms have higher error rates for people with darker skin tones, particularly women of color. This bias can lead to false identifications and wrongful arrests, as seen in the case of Robert Williams, a Black man who was wrongfully arrested due to a faulty facial recognition match. Such incidents underscore the need for rigorous testing and auditing of AI systems to detect and correct biases before they cause harm.

Another area where AI bias can have severe consequences is in healthcare. AI algorithms are being developed to diagnose diseases, recommend treatments, and predict patient outcomes. However, if these algorithms are trained on datasets that are not representative of diverse populations, they may provide less accurate or harmful recommendations for underrepresented groups. For instance, an AI system trained primarily on data from white patients may not accurately predict the risk of certain diseases for patients of color, leading to delayed diagnoses and poorer health outcomes.

Developing and implementing techniques for bias detection and mitigation in AI systems is crucial to address these challenges. This can involve using more diverse and representative training data, employing algorithmic fairness techniques to ensure equitable treatment of different groups, and conducting regular audits and assessments to identify and correct biases. It is also essential to involve diverse teams of developers, data scientists, and ethics experts in creating and overseeing AI systems to bring various perspectives and catch potential biases.

Moreover, addressing AI bias requires a broader

societal commitment to fairness and non-discrimination. This means ensuring that AI systems are unbiased and actively using AI to identify and combat bias in human decision-making processes. For example, AI algorithms can be used to analyze hiring data and detect patterns of discrimination or to identify and correct biases in judicial sentencing decisions. By using AI to promote fairness and equality, we can work towards a more just and equitable society.

B. Privacy and data security concerns

The development and deployment of AI systems rely heavily on collecting and analyzing vast amounts of data, ranging from personal information and online behavior to biometric data and medical records. While this data can enable powerful AI applications and insights, it raises significant concerns about privacy and data security.

One primary privacy concern with AI is the potential for data misuse and unauthorized access. As more sensitive data is collected and stored by AI systems, there is an increased risk of data breaches, hacks, and leaks that can expose individuals' personal information to bad actors. This can lead to identity theft, financial fraud, and other harms. Sometimes, anonymized or aggregated data can be reverse-engineered to re-identify individuals, compromising their privacy.

Another area for improvement is the need for more transparency and control over how AI systems collect, use, and share personal data. Many people need to be made aware of the extent to which their data is being harvested and analyzed by AI algorithms, and they may need more meaningful options to opt out or control their data. This is particularly concerning when AI systems make essential decisions about individuals, such as hiring, lending, or insurance, without their knowledge or consent.

There are also concerns about AI's potential to enable more pervasive surveillance and tracking of individuals. Facial recognition technology, for example, can identify and track individuals in public spaces without their consent, raising fears of a "Big Brother" society. Similarly, AI-powered analytics can monitor and predict individuals' behavior and preferences, enabling targeted advertising and manipulation.

Developing and enforcing solid data protection regulations and practices is essential to address these privacy and security concerns. This includes requiring companies to obtain explicit consent for data collection and use, providing individuals with clear information about how their data will be used and shared, and allowing them to access, correct, and delete their data. It also means implementing robust security measures to protect against data breaches and unauthorized access, such as encryption, access controls, and regular security audits.

In addition, there is a need for greater transparency and accountability around AI systems that use personal data. Companies should be required to disclose the types of data they collect, how it is used in AI algorithms, and what steps they take to ensure privacy and security. There should also be mechanisms for individuals to challenge and appeal AI-driven decisions that affect them and for regulators to audit and oversee AI systems to ensure compliance with data protection rules.

Balancing AI's benefits with the need for privacy and security will require ongoing collaboration and dialogue between technology companies, policymakers, civil society groups, and individuals. By developing and implementing robust data governance frameworks, we can harness AI's power while protecting individuals' privacy and dignity.

C. Transparency and accountability in AI decision-making

As AI systems become more sophisticated and autonomous, making decisions that can significantly impact individuals and society, ensuring transparency and accountability in their decision-making processes is crucial. With clear explanations of how AI algorithms arrive at their conclusions, it can be easier to trust their outputs or hold them accountable for any harm they may cause.

One major challenge with AI transparency is many machine learning algorithms' "black box" nature. These algorithms can involve complex neural networks with millions of parameters, making it difficult for creators to understand exactly how they arrive at specific decisions. This opacity can make detecting and correcting errors, biases, or unintended consequences in AI systems is challenging.

Moreover, the need for more transparency in AI decision-making can make it difficult for individuals to challenge or appeal decisions that affect them. If someone is denied a loan, job, or benefit due to an AI algorithm, they may need insight into why the decision was made or how to contest it. This can lead to a sense of powerlessness and erode trust in AI systems and the institutions that use them.

To address these challenges, there is a growing movement towards "explainable AI" (XAI), which aims to create AI systems that provide clear and understandable explanations for their decisions. This can involve techniques such as feature importance analysis, which identifies the key factors that influenced a decision, or counterfactual explanations, which show how a decision might have been different under alternative scenarios. XAI can help build trust and accountability in AI systems by making AI decision-making more transparent and interpretable.

Another important aspect of AI accountability is ensuring clear lines of responsibility and liability for AI-driven harms. As AI systems become more autonomous and complex, it can be challenging to determine who is responsible when something goes wrong - the developers who created the algorithm, the company that deployed it, or the users who relied on its outputs. This uncertainty can create a "moral hazard" where actors are not incentivized to ensure the safety and fairness of AI systems.

Transparent legal and regulatory frameworks that assign responsibility and liability for AI-driven harms are needed to address this. This could involve requiring companies to conduct impact assessments and risk analyses before deploying AI systems, mandating regular audits and testing to ensure ongoing safety and fairness, and holding companies liable for any harm caused by their AI products or services. Independent oversight bodies or ombudspersons may also investigate and adjudicate AI-related complaints and disputes.

Ultimately, ensuring transparency and accountability in AI decision-making will require a multi-stakeholder approach that involves developers, companies, policymakers, and the public. By working together to create standards, regulations, and best practices for responsible AI development and deployment, we can build AI systems that are trustworthy, fair, and beneficial to society.

D. Balancing the benefits and risks of AI

As we have seen throughout this chapter, the development and deployment of AI systems come with both immense potential benefits and significant risks and challenges. On the one hand, AI has the potential to revolutionize industries, solve complex problems, and improve human lives in countless ways. On the other hand, AI systems can perpetuate biases, violate privacy, and cause unintended harm if not developed and used responsibly.

Balancing these benefits and risks requires a nuanced and context-specific approach that considers the application of AI, the stakeholders involved, and the potential impacts on individuals and society. In some cases, the benefits of AI outweigh the risks, such as in healthcare applications that can save lives or in scientific research that can accelerate discovery. In other cases, the risks may be too high to justify using AI, such as in military applications that could lead to autonomous weapons or surveillance systems that could enable authoritarian control.

One fundamental principle for balancing AI's benefits and risks is prioritizing human values and ethics throughout development and deployment. This means designing AI systems with fairness, transparency, and accountability in mind from the outset rather than trying to retrofit these considerations afterward. It also means involving diverse stakeholders, including affected communities and domain experts, in the design and governance of AI systems to ensure that they reflect a range of perspectives and values.

Another important consideration is the need for ongoing monitoring, evaluation, and adjustment of AI systems. As AI technologies evolve and are deployed in new contexts, it is essential to continually assess their impacts and make necessary changes to mitigate risks and harms. This may involve regular audits and testing of AI algorithms, as well as mechanisms for affected individuals and communities to provide feedback and input.

Clear guidelines and regulations are also needed to develop and use AI systems. While overly restrictive regulations could stifle innovation and limit AI's potential benefits, a lack of oversight and accountability could lead to unchecked harms and abuses. Striking the right balance will require collaboration between policymakers, industry leaders, civil society groups, and other stakeholders to develop standards and best practices that promote responsible AI development while enabling beneficial applications.

Ultimately, the key to balancing AI's benefits and risks is to approach it with a spirit of humility, caution, and ongoing learning. We must recognize that AI is a powerful tool but one that is not infallible or inherently good. By carefully considering the ethical implications of AI, involving diverse perspectives in its development and governance, and remaining vigilant and adaptable in the face of new challenges, we can work towards a future in which AI benefits humanity while minimizing its potential harm.

VIII. PREPARING FOR AN AI-DRIVEN WORLD

A. Developing AI literacy and skills

As AI technologies become increasingly ubiquitous, touching nearly every aspect of our lives, individuals must develop a foundational understanding of AI concepts, capabilities, and limitations. This "AI literacy" will be essential for navigating an AI-driven world, making informed decisions, and participating in the development and governance of AI systems.

At a basic level, AI literacy involves understanding what AI is, how it works, and what it can and cannot do. This includes familiarity with key concepts such as machine learning, neural networks, and natural language processing and an appreciation for the differences between narrow AI (designed for specific tasks) and general AI (capable of intelligent behavior across multiple domains). It also means being aware of the potential biases, errors, and unintended consequences that can arise in AI systems and knowing how to evaluate AI-generated outputs critically.

Beyond this foundational knowledge, developing AI literacy also requires hands-on experience with AI tools and technologies. This could involve learning to use AI-powered software and platforms, such as machine learning libraries or natural language processing APIs, or even building simple AI models and applications from scratch. By gaining practical experience with AI, individuals can demystify the technology, build confidence in their abilities, and gain a deeper appreciation for the possibilities and challenges of AI development.

Importantly, AI literacy is for more than just technical experts or data scientists. As AI becomes more integrated into various industries and domains, professionals across fields must understand how AI can be applied to their work and how it may change their roles and responsibilities. This means that AI literacy training and education should be available and accessible to everyone, from students and educators to business leaders and policymakers.

Developing AI literacy and skills will require a concerted effort from multiple stakeholders, including educational institutions, employers, and governments. Schools and universities should incorporate AI concepts and skills into their curricula, allowing students to learn about and work with AI technologies. Employers should invest in AI training and upskilling programs for their workers, helping them adapt to AI-driven changes in their industries. Governments should support AI literacy initiatives and ensure that all citizens have access to AI education and resources.

By prioritizing AI literacy and skills development, we can empower individuals to participate actively in the AI revolution rather than be passive bystanders. With a strong foundation of AI knowledge and capabilities, individuals will be better equipped to make informed decisions, contribute to the development of responsible AI systems, and thrive in an AI-driven world.

B. Adapting to AI-driven changes in society

As AI technologies transform industries, economies, and social structures, individuals and communities must adapt to a range of AI-driven societal changes. These changes will bring opportunities and challenges, and successfully navigating them will require flexibility, resilience, and a willingness to learn and evolve.

One central area of AI-driven change will be work and employment. As AI automates specific tasks and roles, some jobs may disappear while others will be created or transformed. Workers must be prepared to continually upskill and reskill throughout their careers, learning new technologies and adapting to shifting job requirements. This may involve pursuing additional education and training and being open to new career paths and industries.

Beyond the workplace, AI will also change how we live, learn, and interact with the world around us. AI-powered personalization and recommendation systems will shape the information and content we consume, our products and services, and the communities we engage with. While this can bring convenience and efficiency, it raises concerns about filter bubbles, manipulation, and loss of privacy. Individuals must be aware of these risks and take steps to maintain a diverse and balanced information diet and protect their data and autonomy.

AI will also profoundly impact social and political structures, potentially exacerbating existing inequalities and creating new forms of discrimination and exclusion. As AI systems are used to make decisions in areas such as hiring, lending, and criminal justice, there is a risk that they will perpetuate and amplify human biases and systemic inequities. Marginalized communities may face additional barriers to accessing and benefiting from AI technologies, widening the digital divide.

To mitigate these risks and ensure that the benefits of AI are widely shared, it will be essential to prioritize diversity, equity, and inclusion in the development and deployment of AI systems. This means actively involving underrepresented groups in the creation and governance of AI, as well as designing AI systems that are fair, transparent, and accountable to the communities they impact. It also means investing in programs and policies that promote digital inclusion and empowerment, such as affordable broadband access, digital literacy training, and community-based AI initiatives.

Adapting to AI-driven societal changes will require ongoing learning, dialogue, and collaboration among diverse stakeholders. Individuals, communities, businesses, and governments will need to work together to anticipate and respond to AI's social, economic, and political impacts while also proactively shaping the development and use of AI technologies to align with human values and priorities. By embracing change and working towards a more just and equitable AI future, we can build a society that harnesses AI's power for the benefit of all.

C. Leveraging AI for personal and professional growth

While the AI revolution presents challenges and uncertainties, it offers immense personal and professional growth opportunities. By proactively learning about and engaging with AI technologies, individuals can position themselves to thrive in an AI-driven world and harness the power of AI for their benefit and advancement.

One key area where individuals can leverage AI for growth is in their careers and professional development. As AI reshapes industries and job markets, those with the skills and knowledge to work with and alongside AI systems will be in high demand. Individuals can open up new career opportunities and command higher salaries by developing expertise in AI-related fields such as data science, machine learning, or natural language processing. Even for those not directly working in AI, understanding how to use AI tools and platforms can enhance productivity, creativity, and decision-making in various roles.

Beyond the workplace, AI can also be a powerful tool for personal growth and self-improvement. AI-powered educational platforms and tutoring systems can provide personalized learning experiences, helping individuals acquire new knowledge and skills more efficiently and effectively. AI coaches and therapists can offer tailored guidance and support for mental health, wellness, and personal development. And AI-generated content and experiences, such as music, art, and virtual reality, can stimulate creativity, imagination, and self-expression.

Another way individuals can leverage AI for growth is by using it to gain insights and make better decisions in various aspects of life. AI-powered financial management tools can help individuals budget, save, and invest more wisely. AI health monitoring devices can provide real-time feedback and recommendations for improving physical and mental well-being. AI predictive analytics can help individuals anticipate and prepare for future challenges and opportunities, from career transitions to major life events.

Of course, leveraging AI for personal and professional growth also requires awareness of the technology's potential risks and limitations. It is essential to approach AI critically and discerningly, recognizing that AI systems can be biased, inaccurate, or manipulative. Individuals should also be mindful of the privacy implications of sharing personal data with AI platforms and take steps to protect their information and autonomy.

Ultimately, the key to leveraging AI for growth is to approach it as a tool and a partner rather than a replacement for human intelligence and agency. By combining the power of AI with uniquely human qualities such as creativity, empathy, and judgment, individuals can amplify their capabilities and achieve new levels of personal and professional fulfillment. With a proactive and purposeful approach to AI, individuals can adapt to an AI-driven world and shape it in positive and transformative ways.

D. Contributing to the responsible development of AI

As AI technologies become more powerful and pervasive, it is crucial that principles of responsibility, ethics, and social good guide their development and deployment. While the primary responsibility for ensuring responsible AI lies with the companies, researchers, and policymakers directly involved in AI development, every individual has a role to play in shaping the future of AI and holding those in positions of power accountable.

Individuals can contribute to responsible AI development by advocating for transparency, fairness, and accountability in AI systems. This could involve supporting policies and regulations that require AI companies to disclose how their algorithms work, test for and mitigate biases, and be held liable for any harms caused by their products. It could also mean using social media and other platforms to raise awareness about AI issues and pressure companies and governments to act in the public interest.

Another vital way individuals can contribute is by participating in the development and governance of AI systems. This could involve joining community advisory boards or stakeholder groups that provide input into the design and deployment of AI in local contexts, such as in schools, hospitals, or government agencies. It could also mean engaging in public deliberation and dialogue around AI's social and ethical implications through forums such as citizen assemblies, online discussions, or town hall meetings.

Individuals with technical skills and expertise can also directly contribute to the development of responsible AI by working on projects and initiatives that prioritize ethics, safety, and social impact. This could include contributing to open-source AI tools and datasets designed with transparency and accountability in mind or collaborating with interdisciplinary teams to develop AI solutions for pressing social and environmental challenges. It could also involve conducting research on the social and ethical dimensions of AI and developing new methods and frameworks for responsible AI development.

Individuals without technical backgrounds can support responsible AI development by advocating for diversity and inclusion in the AI field. This means promoting STEM education and career pathways for underrepresented groups, such as women, people of color, and individuals from low-income backgrounds. It also means challenging biases and discrimination within AI companies and research institutions and supporting initiatives to create more equitable and inclusive AI ecosystems.

Ultimately, contributing to responsible AI development requires a collective effort from individuals across all sectors of society. It means staying informed about AI issues and developments, voicing concerns and ideas, and taking action to hold those in power accountable. It also means recognizing that the development of AI is not just a technical challenge but also a social and political one with profound implications for the future of humanity.

As we move forward into an AI-driven world, we all must take responsibility for shaping the trajectory of this transformative technology. By working together to ensure that AI is developed and used in ways that benefit everyone, we can create a future in which the power of AI is harnessed for the greater good and the benefits of this technology are shared equitably across society. With a commitment to responsible AI development, we can build a world in which AI enhances rather than replaces human potential and in which the promise of this technology is realized in service of a more just, sustainable, and flourishing future for all.

IX. CASE STUDIES AND SUCCESS STORIES

A. Individuals who have harnessed AI for personal growth

Throughout this book, we've explored how AI is transforming industries, economies, and societies. But AI is not just a tool for businesses and governments; it also has the power to transform the lives of individuals in profound and meaningful ways. In this section, we'll examine some inspiring stories of people who have harnessed AI for personal growth and self-improvement.

One such individual is Sarah, a 35-year-old marketing executive who struggled with anxiety and depression for years. Despite trying various therapies and medications, she always felt like she was just managing her symptoms rather than genuinely overcoming her challenges. That changed when Sarah discovered an AI-powered mental health app that used machine learning to provide personalized cognitive-behavioral therapy (CBT) exercises and mood tracking.

By engaging with the app daily and using its insights to identify patterns in her thoughts and behaviors, Sarah was able to gain a deeper understanding of her mental health and develop more effective coping strategies. The app's AI algorithms also adapted to her unique needs and preferences, providing increasingly tailored recommendations and support. Within a few months, Sarah noticed a significant improvement in her anxiety and depression symptoms, and she felt more in control of her mental well-being than ever before.

Another inspiring example is Mark, a 50-year-old factory worker who had always dreamed of starting his own business but felt held back by his lack of formal education and technical skills. When his employer announced plans to automate parts of the manufacturing process using AI and robotics, Mark saw an opportunity to learn new skills and redefine his career path.

He enrolled in an online AI and machine learning course, which used adaptive learning algorithms to personalize the content and pacing to his individual needs and abilities. Mark also participated in a virtual mentorship program connecting him with experienced AI professionals who provided guidance and support as he developed his AI projects and business ideas.

With his newfound knowledge and confidence,

Mark could transition into a new role as an AI consultant for manufacturing companies, helping them optimize their processes and train their workers on the latest technologies. He also launched a side business developing custom AI solutions for small and medium-sized enterprises, quickly gaining traction and allowing him to pursue his entrepreneurial dreams.

These are just two examples of the many ways in which individuals are using AI to unlock their potential and achieve their goals. By leveraging the power of personalized learning, predictive analytics, and intelligent decision support, people from all walks of life are finding new opportunities for growth, fulfillment, and success in an AI-driven world.

B. Companies that have successfully integrated AI into their operations

While AI can transform individual lives, it is also revolutionizing how companies operate and compete in the global marketplace. Across industries and sectors, forward-thinking organizations are harnessing the power of AI to drive innovation, efficiency, and customer value. Here are a few notable examples:

One company that has successfully integrated AI into its operations is Ocado, a British online supermarket and technology firm. Ocado has developed a highly automated warehousing and logistics system that uses AI and robotics to pick, pack, and deliver groceries quickly and accurately. Ocado has achieved industry-leading efficiency and customer satisfaction by leveraging machine learning algorithms to optimize inventory management, route planning, and customer service.

Another example is Ant Group, a Chinese fintech company that has used AI to transform how financial services are delivered to underserved populations. Ant Group's AI-powered mobile payment and lending platforms have enabled millions of small businesses and individuals to access credit and participate in the digital economy without traditional banking infrastructure. By using machine learning to assess risk and personalize offerings, Ant Group has provided affordable and accessible financial services to previously excluded groups.

Companies like Babylon Health and Deepmind use AI to improve patient outcomes and reduce costs in the healthcare sector. Babylon Health's AI-powered chatbot and telemedicine platform have made it easier for patients to access medical advice and treatment remotely. Machine learning assists doctors in diagnosing and treating conditions. Deepmind's AI algorithms have been used to predict patient deterioration, optimize hospital resource allocation, and even discover new drugs and therapies.

These are just a few examples of the many companies successfully integrating AI into their operations and reaping the benefits of increased efficiency, innovation, and customer value. As more organizations adopt and scale AI technologies, we expect to see even more transformative impacts across industries and sectors.

C. AI-driven innovations that have transformed industries

Beyond individual companies, AI is also driving broader industry-wide transformations that reshape entire sectors and create new growth and innovation opportunities. Here are a few examples of AI-driven innovations that have had a profound impact on their respective industries:

In the transportation industry, the development of autonomous vehicles has the potential to revolutionize the way people and goods are moved around. Companies like Tesla, Waymo, and Uber use AI and machine learning to develop self-driving cars and trucks that can navigate complex environments with human-like perception and decision-making capabilities. As autonomous vehicle technology matures and becomes more widely adopted, it could lead to significant improvements in safety, efficiency, and accessibility of transportation.

In the energy sector, AI is used to optimize the production and distribution of renewable energy sources like wind and solar power. Using machine learning algorithms to predict weather patterns, energy demand, and grid performance, companies like DeepMind and Autogrid are helping utilities integrate renewable energy sources more efficiently and cost-effectively. This helps reduce greenhouse gas emissions, combat climate change, and create new opportunities for innovation and growth in the clean energy industry.

In retail, AI transforms how companies interact with customers and personalize their offerings. Companies like Amazon and Alibaba use machine learning algorithms to analyze customer data and provide tailored product recommendations, dynamic pricing, and targeted marketing. By leveraging AI to create more personalized and engaging shopping experiences, these companies drive significant improvements in customer loyalty, conversion rates, and revenue growth.

These are just a few examples of how AI is transforming industries and creating new opportunities for innovation and growth. As AI technologies continue to advance and mature, we can expect to see even more disruptive and transformative impacts across sectors in the years to come.

D. Inspiring examples of AI's positive impact on society

While much of the discussion around AI focuses on its economic and business impacts, it's essential to recognize how AI is also being used to address social and environmental challenges and improve people's lives. Here are a few inspiring examples of AI's positive impact on society:

One organization that is using AI for social good is Thorn, a non-profit that leverages technology to combat child sexual abuse and exploitation. Thorn has developed an AI-powered tool called Spotlight that helps law enforcement agencies identify and locate victims of sexual abuse more quickly and efficiently. By using machine learning algorithms to analyze massive amounts of online data and detect patterns of abuse, Spotlight has helped to rescue thousands of children and bring perpetrators to justice.

Another example is WattTime, a startup that is using AI to reduce greenhouse gas emissions from the electricity sector. WattTime has developed a machine learning algorithm that analyzes real-time data from the power grid and predicts when renewable energy sources like wind and solar will be available. By providing this information to consumers and businesses, WattTime enables them to shift their energy usage to times when clean energy is most abundant, thereby reducing their carbon footprint and supporting the transition to a low-carbon economy.

AI improves access to care and support for underserved populations in the healthcare sector. One example is the Mila chatbot, developed by the South African non-profit organization mothers2mothers. Mila uses natural language processing and machine learning to provide personalized health information and support to HIV-positive mothers in sub-Saharan Africa. By offering 24/7 access to accurate and confidential advice, Mila helps to reduce mother-to-child transmission of HIV and improve maternal and child health outcomes.

These are just a few examples of the many ways in which AI is being used to address social and environmental challenges and make a positive impact on people's lives. As more organizations and individuals recognize the potential of AI for social good, we can expect to see even more innovative and impactful applications of this technology in the years to come.

From personal growth and self-improvement to business transformation and social impact, the case studies and success stories showcased in this chapter demonstrate the incredible potential of AI to drive positive change and create value for individuals, organizations, and society as a whole. As we continue to develop and harness the power of AI in responsible and ethical ways, we have the opportunity to build a more prosperous, sustainable, and equitable future for all.

X. CONCLUSION

A. Recap of the key points covered in the book

Throughout this book, we have embarked on a journey to explore the transformative power of Artificial Intelligence and its potential to revolutionize our lives. We began by understanding the fundamentals of AI, tracing its history and evolution from the earliest days of computing to today's cutting-edge developments. We explored the different types of AI, from narrow and general to superintelligent, and examined the current state of AI technology across various domains and applications.

We then delved into how AI is already transforming our daily lives, from the virtual assistants in our homes and pockets to the intelligent systems powering our cars, appliances, and devices. We saw how AI revolutionized education and learning, healthcare and wellness, and countless other aspects of our personal and professional lives.

Moving beyond the individual level, we explored the profound impact of AI on businesses and industries, from automating routine tasks and optimizing operations to enhancing customer experiences and driving innovation. We saw how AI enables new forms of creativity and problem-solving and is poised to reshape the future of work and entrepreneurship.

However, we also grappled with AI's complex ethical considerations and challenges, from bias and fairness to concerns around privacy, security, and accountability. We examined the need for responsible and inclusive AI development and the role that each of us can play in shaping the future of this powerful technology.

Through inspiring case studies and success stories, we witnessed AI's incredible potential to transform lives and drive positive change. From individuals using AI for personal growth and self-improvement to companies and organizations harnessing its power for business transformation and social impact, we saw the myriad ways AI is already creating value and unlocking human potential.

B. The importance of embracing AI as a tool for empowerment

As seen throughout this book, AI is not just another technological trend or fad. It is a fundamentally transformative force reshaping our world profoundly and more far-reaching. As such, we must approach AI not with fear or trepidation but with a spirit of curiosity, openness, and empowerment.

At its core, AI is a powerful and sophisticated tool, but it is nonetheless a tool. Like any tool, its impact and value depend on how we wield it. When used responsibly and ethically, AI has the potential to amplify our abilities, expand our possibilities, and help us achieve things that were once thought impossible.

But to truly harness the power of AI, we must first embrace it as a tool for empowerment. This means recognizing that AI is not here to replace us but to augment and enhance our capabilities. It means seeing AI not as a threat to our jobs or ways of life but as an opportunity to create new forms of value, meaning, and fulfillment.

Embracing AI as a tool for empowerment also means taking an active role in shaping its development and deployment. It means staying informed about AI's latest advancements and applications and engaging in ongoing conversations and collaborations around its ethical and social implications. It means advocating for responsible and inclusive AI practices and holding those in positions of power accountable for their actions and decisions.

Ultimately, embracing AI as a tool for empowerment means recognizing that the future is not something that happens to us but something that we create together. By proactively engaging with AI and harnessing its potential for good, we can shape a more just, sustainable, and fulfilling future for all.

C. A call to action for readers to explore and harness the power of AI

If there is one message that readers will take away from this book, it is this: the power of AI is not something to be feared or ignored but something to be explored, harnessed, and leveraged for personal and collective growth.

Whether you are a business leader looking to drive innovation and efficiency, an entrepreneur seeking to launch the next game-changing startup, or simply an individual looking to unlock your full potential, AI has something to offer you. But to truly benefit from this incredible technology, you must take action.

So here is my call to action for you, dear reader: start exploring AI today. Take a course, attend a workshop, or join a community of like-minded learners and innovators. Experiment with AI tools and platforms and build your projects and applications. Seek out mentors and collaborators who can guide and support you on your journey.

But don't stop there. As you deepen your knowledge and skills in AI, look for ways to apply them to the challenges and opportunities that matter most to you. Whether using AI to improve your life and work or leveraging it to drive social and environmental impact, there are countless ways to harness the power of this technology for good.

As you do so, remember to approach AI with a spirit of responsibility, ethics, and inclusivity. Use your knowledge and skills to help create a future that is not only more prosperous and innovative but also more just and equitable for all.

D. The potential for AI to shape a better future for all

As we look to the future, it is clear that AI will play an increasingly central role in shaping our world. From transforming industries and economies to enhancing our cognitive and physical capabilities, AI's potential applications and impacts are both vast and profound.

However, as we have seen throughout this book, the future of AI is not fixed or predetermined. We must actively create and shape a future together through our choices, actions, and values.

Suppose we approach AI with empowerment, responsibility, and inclusivity. In that case, we can harness its incredible potential to drive positive change and create a better world. We can use AI to solve the most significant challenges of our time, from climate change and disease to poverty and inequality. We can leverage it to unlock new forms of creativity, discovery, and human potential. We can also ensure that its benefits are shared equitably and its risks are mitigated effectively.

But if we approach AI with fear, ignorance, or apathy, we risk missing out on these incredible opportunities or exacerbating the problems we seek to solve. We risk creating a future in which AI is used to entrench existing power structures and inequalities or to harm and exploit the most vulnerable among us.

The choice is ours. As individuals and as a society, we have the power to shape the future of AI and the future of our world. By embracing AI as a tool for empowerment, by taking action to explore and harness its potential, and by working together to ensure its responsible and ethical development, we can create a future that is not only more innovative and prosperous but also more just, sustainable, and fulfilling for all.

So, let us go forth with courage, curiosity, and compassion. Let us embrace AI's power to transform our lives and our world for the better. Let us work together to build a future in which this technology's incredible potential is fully realized in service of our highest aspirations and deepest values.

The journey ahead will not be easy but it will be filled with opportunity, discovery, and growth. With the power of AI at our fingertips and the strength of our collective wisdom and will, there is no limit to what we can achieve.

The future is ours to create. Let us begin.

THEODOREBRISTOL

ΔΔΔ

www.ingramcontent.com/pod-product-compliance
Lightning Source LLC
Chambersburg PA
CBHW070346230526
45471CB00006B/2437